EARLY AMERICAN FURNITURE

By KEVIN CALLAHAN

Weathervane Books • New York

Copyright © MCMLXXV by Kevin Callahan

Library of Congress Catalog Card Number: 76-4519

This edition is published by Weathervane Books
a division of Imprint Society, Inc.,
distributed by Crown Publishers, Inc.
by arrangement with Drake Publishers, Inc.
a   b   c   d   e   f   g   h

To my wife Carmel,
who helped with the
research and kept my
coffee cup filled.

Acknowledgments

I would like to thank Bob Walin of Half-House Antiques in Woodbury, Connecticut and Jim Bok of Fairfield, Conn. for letting me wander about their homes and shops, sketch book in hand, drawing both their merchandise and personal possessions. Also, Ralph Bloom, curator of the Lockwood House Museum in Norwalk, Connecticut for allowing me to sketch some of the fine pieces in the museum collection.

I've written this book to give the novice collector some insight into the field of early American country furniture from the 18th century until about 1840. Most of the items illustrated aren't museum pieces, but pieces I own or have owned at one time; others belong to friends who were kind enough to let me come into their homes and sketch their furniture.

Country furniture is informal, but certainly not primitive, although it was made outside the major style centers of the day, it has a style and a strength all its own. The woods used were the native woods found in the area, chiefly maple, cherry, pine and walnut.

It was sturdy furniture, made for

daily use and a surprising amount of it has survived and remains in daily use two hundred years later, a fact which surely speaks well of the early furniture makers. (where will the stapled together plastic laminated furniture of the 1970's be two hundred years from now?)

Perhaps the best way to illustrate the difference between urban furniture and country furniture is to give an example of how two craftsmen, one working in a major city, the other in a small farm community might handle the same assignment or as it was called, bespoke work.

A cabinetmaker in Boston, Newport or Philadelphia would make say, a

Chippendale chair that closely followed Thomas Chippendale's latest book of chair design from England. He would select the finest imported mahogany from the stock he kept on hand and using all his skill with saw, chisel and carving tools, would produce a masterpiece of the chairmaker's art.

Our friend in the country, not having a copy of Chippendale's book, but following a remembered example in his minds' eye, with his own ideas on chair design tossed in for good measure and working in perhaps curly maple, would produce a simplified version of the same chair with a character and charm all it's own.

Today the mahogany example is probably in a museum. Even if it isn't, most of us couldn't afford to buy it. The price would be more than you probably paid for your house.

The country example is another story, since most people can fit a few good pieces into there budget.

Remember, you're not just buying furniture, but investing in a commodity whose supply is dwindling and whose price is constantly rising.

CONTENTS

ACKNOWLEDGEMENTS.................

PREFACE................................

1. Where to look 1-5

2. Chairs-18th to the 19th century..........6-29

3. Windsor Chairs 30-35

4. Tables 36-57

5. Case Furniture 58-88
   furniture brasses, chests
   desks, cupboards

6. Cabinetmakers Tools 89-92

7. Advertising Broadside............93-94

8. Refinishing and minor repairs.....95-111

9. Accessories........................112-158
   Tinware, Lighting Devices, Warmers, Foodsafe
   Ironware, Woodenware, Boxes, Mirrors
   Clocks, Stoneware

EARLY AMERICAN FURNITURE

The art of acquiring period furniture is really quite simple if you have a six figure income. All you do is go to the best shop in any major city in the world, make out a list, and have the stuff delivered to your home. But, if like most of us you're a few zeros short of six in the income department, then you'll have to get out and do some hunting. Which brings us to the reason for writing this chapter in the first place, that is, where to hunt.

Auction buying is lots of fun, an evening out away from the kids and a good way to buy at true market value. But it's also fraught with danger for the uninformed.

As far as most auctioneers are concerned if "you bought it, you own it," so it pays to know what your buying before you stick your hand in the air.

The caveat emptor style of auction buying requires that you attend the auction preview, usually held an hour or two before the start of the actual auction. This allows you to examine the pieces you're interested in, decide what you're willing to pay and to firm up your resolve not to go above that.

Try not to get caught up in the excitement of the moment, or like New Year's Eve, you'll be sorry in the morning.

The best way I know of to keep informed of important auctions of antique furniture in the north-east is through the Newtown Bee, a weekly newspaper published in Newton Connecticut. It's an informative antique journal well worth subscribing to.

The next most obvious place to look for antique furniture is in the many shops that line the highways and byways of practically every city and town in the country. Be prepared to do some searching though, not many shops these days have as much as one piece of furniture that pre-dates 1840. As a matter of fact many of the so called antiques they carry are items that were common place in this century. I'm sorry, but I can't accept the fact that the Atwater-Kent radio on which I listened to Jack Armstrong is now an antique.

The one advantage to looking in this

kind of shop as well as second hand stores and thrift shops is that if you ever do find a piece of antique furniture you can usually buy it at a bargain price, because most of these dealers wouldn't know an antique if it came up and bit them.

In the final analysis, antiques are where you find them, which often as not is in some unlikely place. I'm sure not a day goes by that somebody, some - where doesn't buy a highboy or a rare piece of pewter at a neighborhood garage sale. But, there are no secret places these days where antiques are practically given away. If you went up and knocked on the door of the most remote farmhouse in the most remote section of the state of Maine to inquire about that nice windsor arm chair on the porch, you would find that a dozen people had been there before you and the farmer is accepting only written bids.

The secret, my friend, is knowing what to look for, being able to detect the spurious from the genuine and the original from the reproduction.

CHAIRS

You may reasonably expect to find more chairs than other antique furniture. If a household had only one table, chances are, given the size of the families at the time, there would have been six, eight or more chairs to accomodate everyone.

Chairs, beginning with the Pilgrim century (very rare) through the 1840's (fairly common) are available in a bewildering variety of styles. I have tried, in the pages that follow, to give you a basic idea of the chair forms that appeared in given time periods. These periods, of course, overlapped, and the further away from the centers of commerce and affluence, consequently the centers of style, the longer a particular style would be in continuous use.

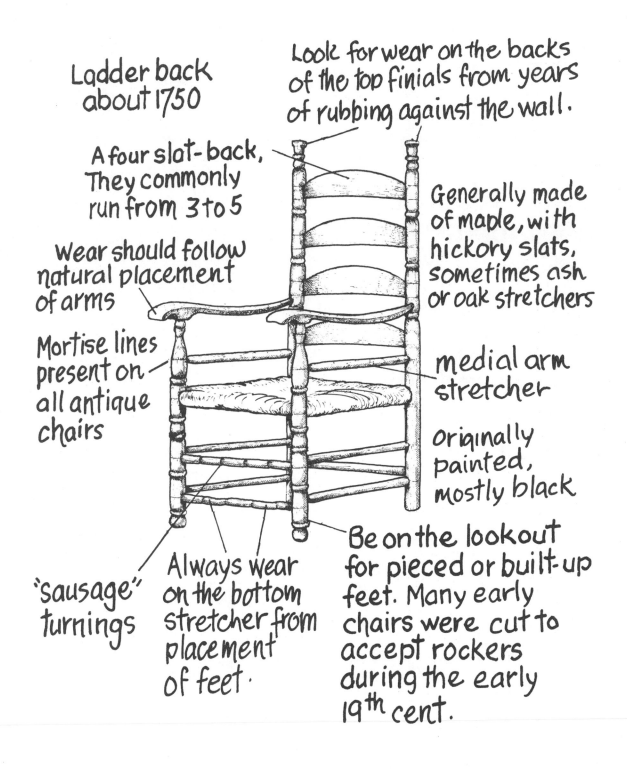

Ladder back
about 1750

Look for wear on the backs
of the top finials from years
of rubbing against the wall.

A four slat-back,
They commonly
run from 3 to 5

Wear should follow
natural placement
of arms

Generally made
of maple, with
hickory slats,
sometimes ash
or oak stretchers

Mortise lines
present on
all antique
chairs

medial arm
stretcher

Originally
painted,
mostly black

"sausage"
turnings

Always wear
on the bottom
stretcher from
placement
of feet.

Be on the lookout
for pieced or built-up
feet. Many early
chairs were cut to
accept rockers
during the early
19th cent.

7

Connecticut
River Valley
Chair
about 1720

An unusual, and early
chair of about 1720.
Discovered only a few
years ago
in a Conn.
farmhouse.
Maple and
Chestnut,
with a well
developed
Spanish
foot.

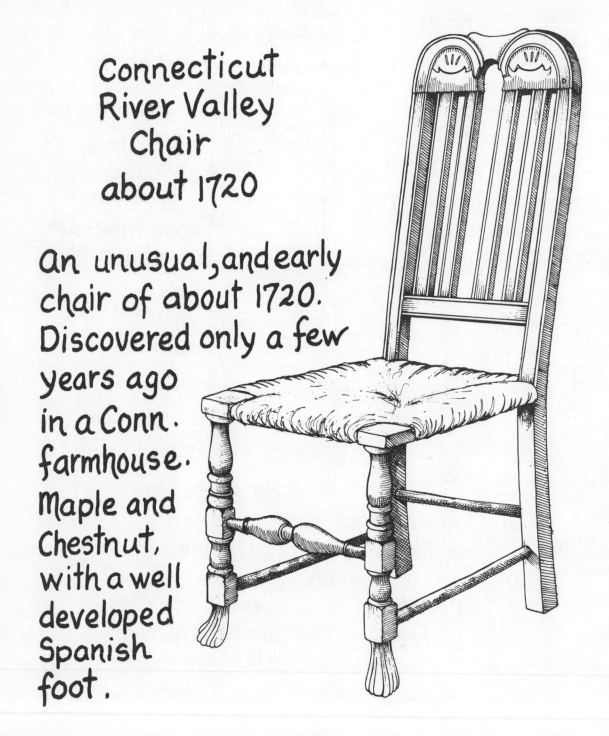

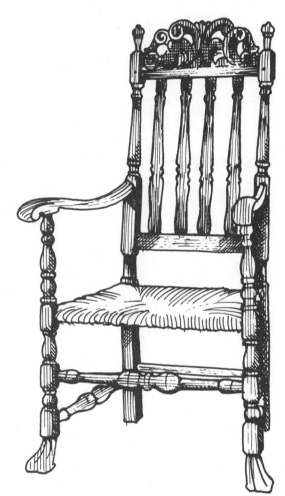

Bannister
back arm chair
early 18th cent.

A spanish foot
chair, of the highest
style. Elegantly
carved crest. Most
bannister back
chairs available
these days are far simpler in style,
the great chairs such as this have
found their way into museums or
outstanding private collections.

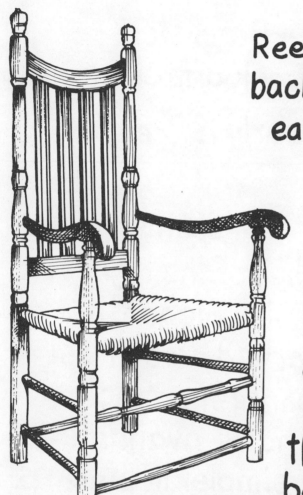

Reeded bannister
back arm chair
early 18th cent.

A Connecticut
chair, with reeded
bannisters, rush
seat, finished in
old dark green
paint. Although
the turned, split
bannister was also
used in Connecticut, the reeded
type has come to be accepted as
a Connecticut style.

Pine settle
early 18thcent.

A simple pine
settle of the
first quarter
of the 18th cent. The seat
lifts for storage. Some of the
early settles were more elaborate,
with paneled backs and heavy moldings.

There are known examples where
the seat folds out into a bed,
preceding the convertible sofa
by a few hundred years.

New England
ladder back side chair
early to mid 18th cent.

A fairly typical,
but nonetheless well
turned ladder back.
The chair retains
much of its' old
black paint.

The ladder back,
with regional differences was
made in all settled parts of the
country from the mid 17th cent.
on.

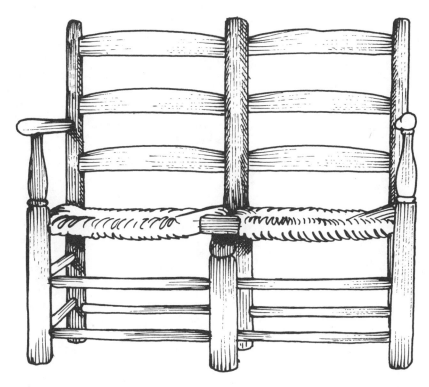

Ladder back wagon seat - 18th cent.

Actually used as extra seating in a wagon, then taken out and put in the house or stored, when it wasn't needed. The heavy center post was for the two rungs, side by side, required for the seat rushing. The wood used was maple.

Queen Anne spoon back
early 18th cent.

A black, painted maple
chair with a rush seat.
Boldly turned front
stretcher and button
foot. The spanish
foot was also
popular in this
period and I
show a sketch
of one here.
This type of foot was not
turned on the lathe, but was
doweled on later.

Country Queen Anne
side chair - 1760

A boldly turned chair
with unusual front leg
turnings and a ball
turned into the middle of
the back posts. The
original finish is a
faded burnt
orange.

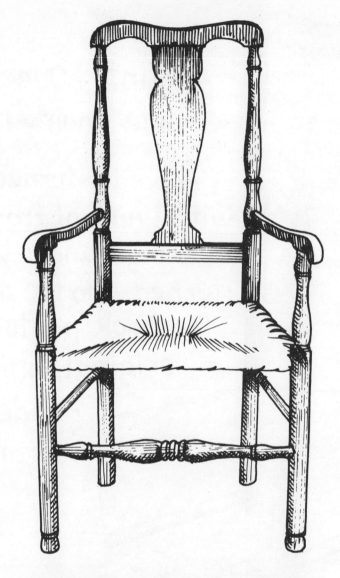

Country Queen Anne
Armchair 1750-65
New England

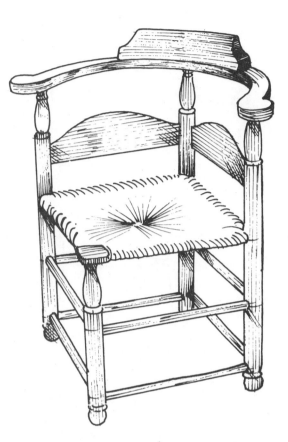

Corner chair
New England
about 1750-60

maple construction
rush seat

Transitional Chippendale
side chair mid 18th cent.

Cherrywood was used
throughout in this Connecticut
chair. It retains the earlier
style below the seat with
the Chippendale back.

Country Queen Anne
So called Hudson Valley type,
found in the New York, Long
Island area - about 1770-80

Philadelphia
type-about
1760

Chippendale
ladder back
1770-80
Connecticut
All cherry

Country
Hepplewhite
about 1790

Cherry, painted black
with an upholstered
seat.

19

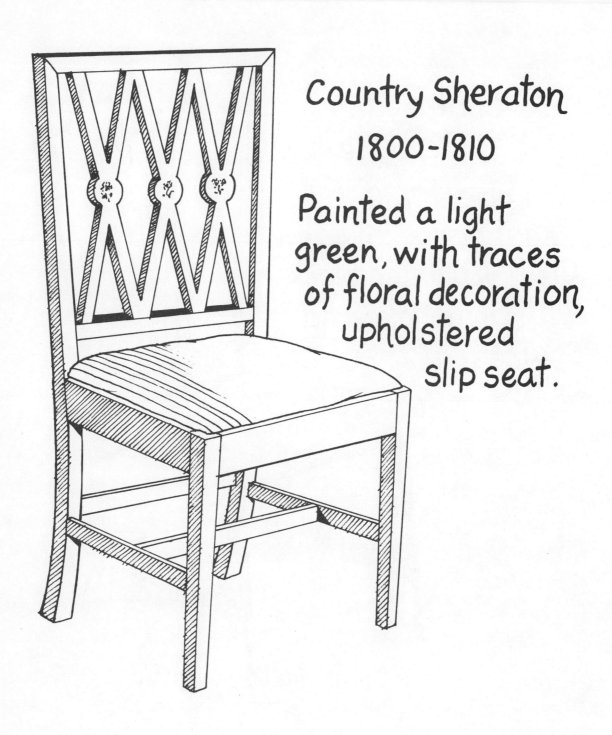

Country Sheraton
1800-1810

Painted a light
green, with traces
of floral decoration,
upholstered
slip seat.

Baby ladder back – about 1780

The front posts on this little ladder back are worn practically flat from being pushed about the floor by generations of little people.

The finish is a well worn green paint.

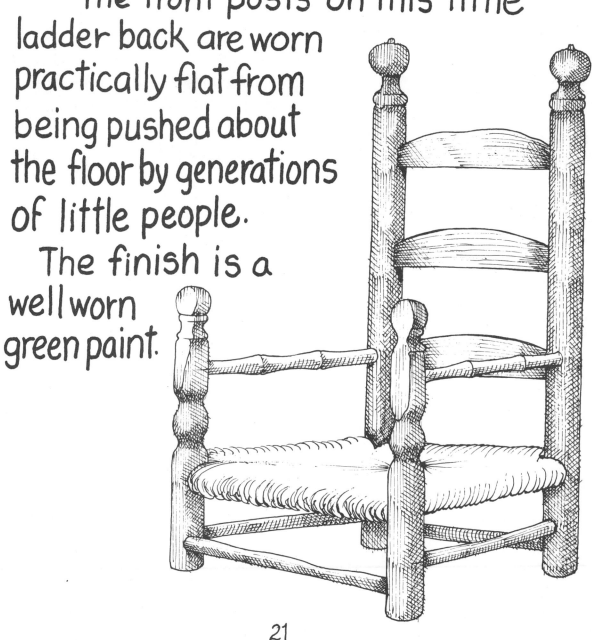

Baby settle chair-18thcent.

All pine construction, simply nailed up with rosehead nails and finished in a grey milk paint, this little chair served a practical purpose which I will assume is obvious to all.

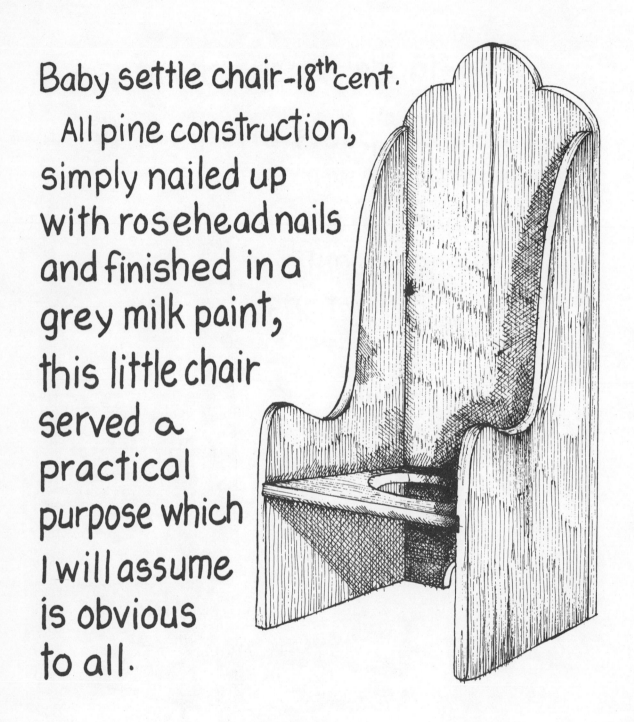

Sheraton Fancy Chair - about 1815

This chair is yellow with a dark green stripe and a free-hand floral decoration on the top slat. The seat on most fancy chairs is rush, but a finer type than you would find on a ladder back chair, for instance.

Hitchcock chair - about 1830

A typical Hitchcock chair, signed
with a stencil on the back of the seat,
HITCHCOCK, ALFORD AND CO. HITCHCOCKS-VILLE CONN.
WARRANTED

These chairs are still being made in
the same place and in much the same
manner as the old chairs.

Boston Rocker 1825-30
made by the Union Chair Co.
Winsted, Conn.

The ubiquitous Boston rocker loved by the novice, scorned by the advanced collector. Unjustly so, I believe, as they are a comfortable, attractive chair that blends well with earlier furniture.

The usual Boston rocker was painted black and striped in yellow, with the decoration on the crest stencilled in bronze powders.

Occasionally you'll see one in yellow, they are more in demand and bring a higher price.

Boston Rockers can be dated by the style of the crest.

before 1835

after 1835

child's
Boston Rocker
about 1840

signed
R·H· Pickett

This little rocker was made in Ridgefield, Conn. by a local cabinet-maker. It's finished in the typical Boston Rocker colors of black and yellow with bronze powders used for the stencilled scene on the crest.

Thumb Back
Windsor High chair
about 1820

The term thumb-
back refers
to the flattened
shape of the
back posts.

28

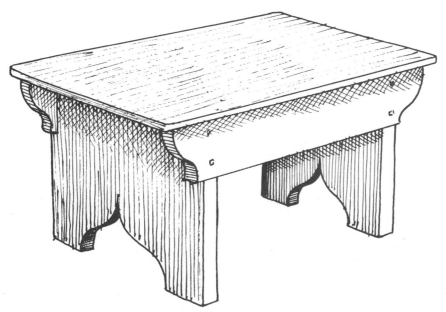

Cricket Stools - Top: 18th cent.
Bottom: early 19th cent.
painted and
decorated.

Windsor Chairs

Although a form of Windsor existed in England, the American version is much lighter in feeling. This is due primarily to the use of ash and hickory for the bent members and spindles of these chairs. With these woods a new lightness developed that is not found in the English chairs of oak and yew wood.

WINDSOR LEG STYLES

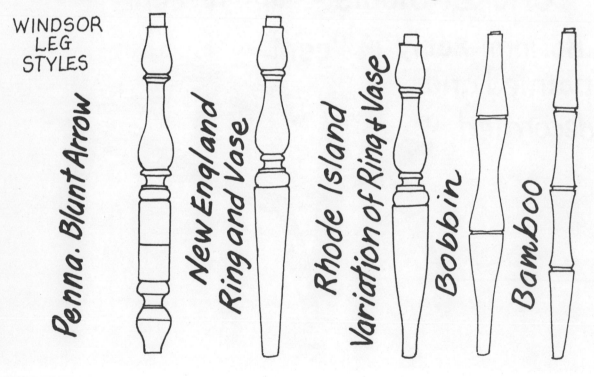

Penna. Blunt Arrow

New England Ring and Vase

Rhode Island Variation of Ring & Vase

Bobbin

Bamboo

Bow-back windsor arm
chair, with comb, about 1780.
Sometimes called a
triple back.

Spindles
are not
added on,
but continue
through the
bow back

Always a one
piece pine
seat. The
tops of the
legs show
through the
seat and are
made fast
with a
wedge.

Scribe marks
are present on
all windsors as
well as other chairs.

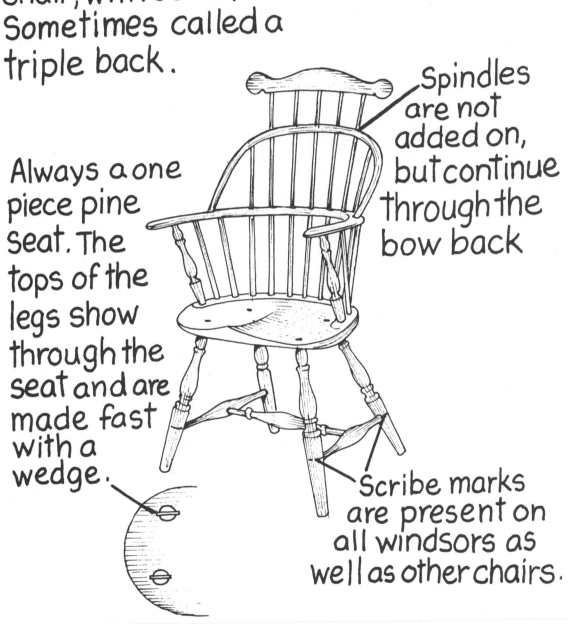

Writing arm Windsor
1760-1770

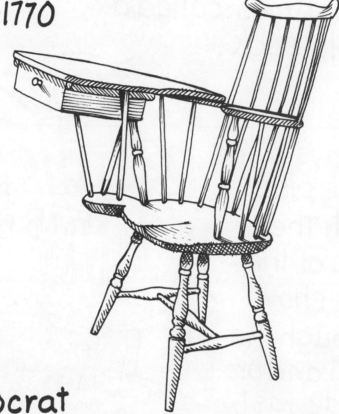

The aristocrat
of Windsor chairs. Rare, beautiful
and expensive, writing arms were
made thoroughout the Windsor period.
The most successful adaptation is
probably the comb back type shown here.

32

Continuous arm Windsor
latter half of the 18th cent.

A very graceful style,
but I've rarely seen one
that wasn't broken at the
point where the arm
bends.

Fan back
Windsor side chair
1760-80

This chair features a well
shaped saddle seat and a
wide splay to the legs.

Bow back with knuckle arm
about 1770

A well turned bow
back arm chair, with
knuckle endings to the
arm. The turnings are
typical of New England and
are called vase and ring.

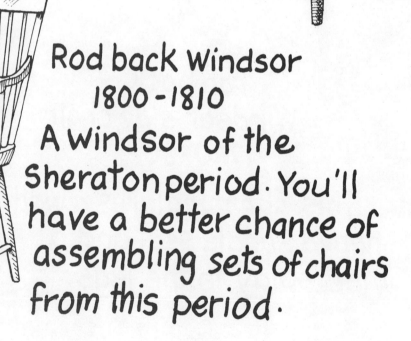

Rod back Windsor
1800-1810

A Windsor of the
Sheraton period. You'll
have a better chance of
assembling sets of chairs
from this period.

34

Arrow back
Windsor arm
chair
1815 -1820

An unusually
large arm chair
that retains its
original dark
green paint
with yellow striping. The
front legs are turned in the bamboo
style. The odd contrivance on the
seat is original and I can offer
no reasonable explanation
for it. Perhaps used to tie it
to the bulkhead on a ship.

IRON STRAP

TABLES

Every household can use a few old tables, the larger ones make charming country dining tables (make sure they haven't lost too much height.) Candlestands are great for resting your coffee cup on next to your favorite easy chair. Yesterday's bedside tables are as well suited to that purpose now as then (better actually, they were certainly put together with more care and pride.)

Most of the old tables you'll see are as sturdy as the day they left the shop or can be put right with some minor gluing and refinishing. Many of the later antique tables are available at prices lower than you would expect to pay for an inferior reproduction.

Tavern table of New England origin. These tables were made from native hardwoods, maple and cherry being common for the base, native pine for the tops. The base on this table is cherry, with a single board pine top 23" wide. mid 18th cent.

Bread board ends are common on tavern tables to prevent the wide board from warping. Usually frankly nailed to the top.

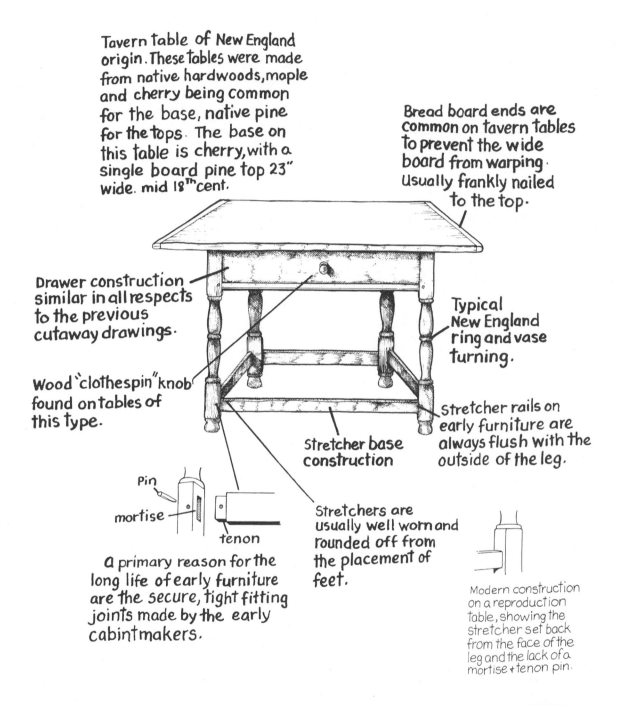

Drawer construction similar in all respects to the previous cutaway drawings.

Wood "clothespin" knob found on tables of this type.

Typical New England ring and vase turning.

Stretcher rails on early furniture are always flush with the outside of the leg.

Stretcher base construction

Pin

mortise

tenon

A primary reason for the long life of early furniture are the secure, tight fitting joints made by the early cabintmakers.

Stretchers are usually well worn and rounded off from the placement of feet.

Modern construction on a reproduction table, showing the stretcher set back from the face of the leg and the lack of a mortise + tenon pin.

37

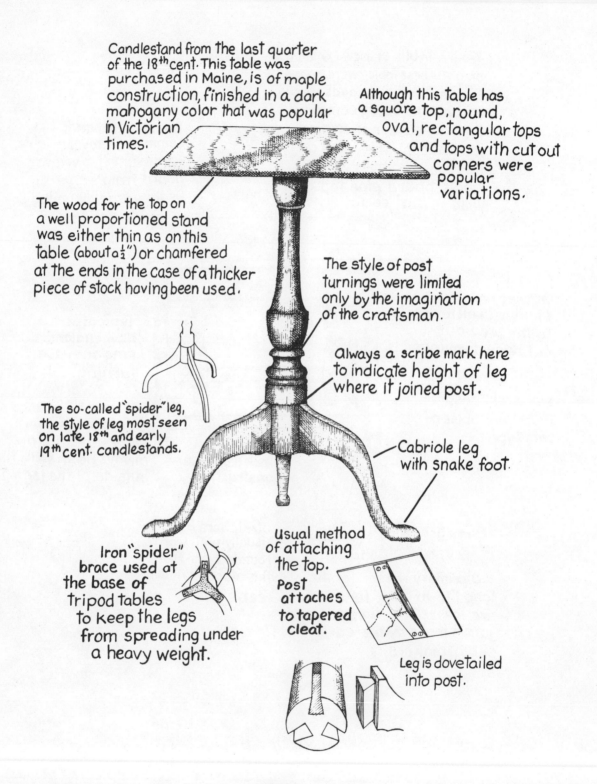

Candlestand from the last quarter of the 18th cent. This table was purchased in Maine, is of maple construction, finished in a dark mahogany color that was popular in Victorian times.

Although this table has a square top, round, oval, rectangular tops and tops with cut out corners were popular variations.

The wood for the top on a well proportioned stand was either thin as on this table (about a ½") or chamfered at the ends in the case of a thicker piece of stock having been used.

The style of post turnings were limited only by the imagination of the craftsman.

Always a scribe mark here to indicate height of leg where it joined post.

The so-called "spider" leg, the style of leg most seen on late 18th and early 19th cent. candlestands.

Cabriole leg with snake foot.

Iron "spider" brace used at the base of tripod tables to keep the legs from spreading under a heavy weight.

Usual method of attaching the top.

Post attaches to tapered cleat.

Leg is dovetailed into post.

Trestle table
17th cent.

The trestle is one of the earliest table forms. This New England table has an oak base, with a pine top that the 17th century housewife scrubbed clean with strong soap after meals.

Pennsylvania
"Sawbuck" Table
early 18th cent.

Top held to the base with pins in
the manner of many early Pennslyvania
tables. Early furniture from this area
has the look of Continental Europe,
unlike the furniture of New England.

Gateleg
  Table
early 18thcent.

Maple gateleg from Northern New England. American gatelegs follow closely the lines of the English tables, although they are lighter in appearance. English gatelegs are invariably oak.

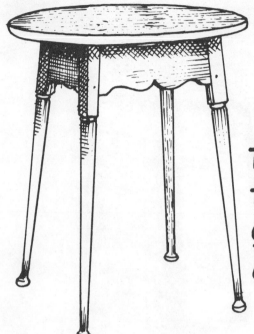

Oval top tea table
mid 18ᵗʰ cent.

Many of these small
tea tables appear on
the market, but the
great demand guarantees
a high price.

Tray top
mid 18ᵗʰ cent.

A Connecticut
cherry table, more
sophisticated in
execution than the
table above.

Small Pine
Table
mid 18th cent.

Scrubbed top, red painted base.

Queen Anne Table
mid 18th cent.

A great country table in the original red paint, pine top and maple base. It's most distinctive feature is, of course, the bold cabriole leg. Found in Bethlehem Connecticut.

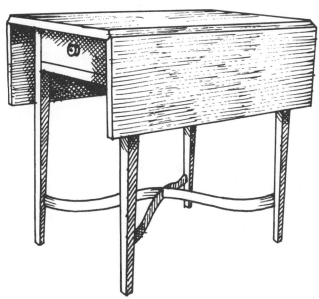

Pembroke Table - about 1790
Serpentine "X" Stretcher

This type of small drop leaf table
was popular from Queen Anne to Empire,
a period of about two hundred years.

They range in style from elegant
examples in Mahogany, with shaped
tops and intricate inlay, to plain country
tables in maple or birch, sometimes
finished in red filler.

Tavern Table
about 1800

Really a survival of the earlier
form. The base is usually maple or
birch finished in red, with a one or
two board pine top.

Painted Table
about 1800-10

Although this country Hepplewhite table dates from the early 19th cent. as does its coat of pale green paint, the elaborately decorated ship painting on the top was done in the early 20th cent. The painting is of the Clipper Red Jacket that went out of service in 1912, and the painting may have been done by someone who sailed on her, to commemorate her passing.

Much country furniture was decorated many years after its construction by a member of the family with artistic talent and time on their hands.

The more charming examples of this folk art are, as you might expect, very much in demand.

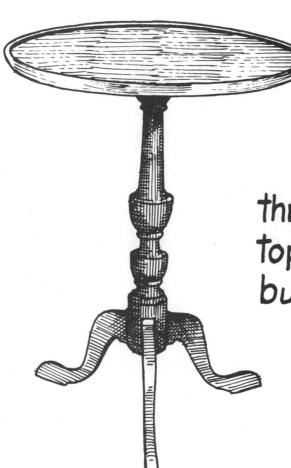

Tripod Table
Circular tray top
1760-1770

Cherry used
throughout, edge on
top is not added,
but turned from the
solid.

Revolving "bird cage"
top, popular in the
same period.

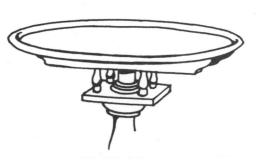

Hepplewhite
Candlestand

Tip-top
"Spider" legs

Top and base, birch.
Was at one time
finished in old red
paint, now in a
natural finish.

One Drawer
Tripod Stand
about 1810-15

Well turned post, all cherry,
with the exception of the curly
maple drawer front, and pine
secondary wood.

Painted Washstand

1815-1820

A piece of bedroom furniture, to hold the washbowl and pitcher. Yellow with dark green stripe.

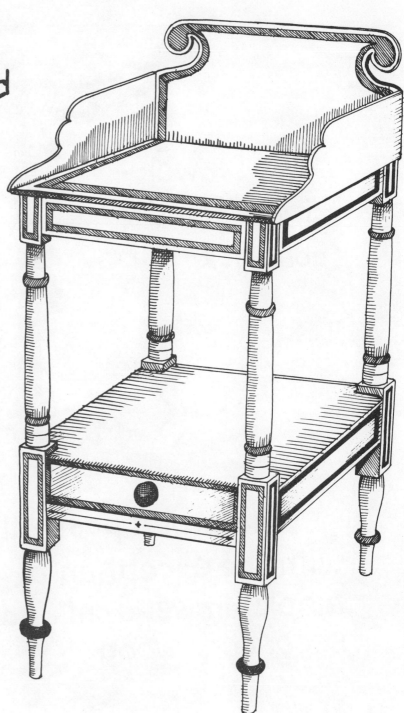

53

Painted Dressing Table
1815-1820

The phenomenal rise in the popularity of early 19th century painted furniture has been matched only by its phenomenal rise in price.

Ten years ago fifty dollars for the dressing table pictured would have made you pause before reaching for your wallet. Today three hundred would be closer to the price and for around two hundred you wouldn't pause at all, but would pay it gladly.

Made by both cabinet makers and early furniture factories, with either free hand or stencilled decoration.

Cherry
One Drawer
Stand

1790-1800

"Turtle" top,
Hepplewhite style
tapered leg.

55

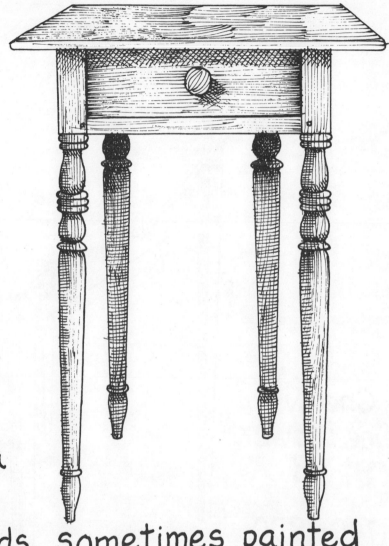

Sheraton
One Drawer
Stand - 1815

Made from a
variety of
native woods, sometimes painted
and decorated. A great many of these
tables come up for sale in shops and
at auction. A slender well turned leg is
an indication of good style.

Doll's Table
mid 19th cent.

A little walnut table
only 12" high and 18" inches long. It's
possibly an apprentice piece or sales-
man's sample. Most full size furniture
had it's counterpart in miniature.

CASE FURNITURE

Under case furniture I've included chests, desks and cupboards, or in other words everything that is basically a wooden case. Some will have a hinged top as the blanket chests, others with drawers, to make a chest of drawers or doors to become cupboards, but still basically a simple wooden case. On the next page you'll find a diagramatical drawing of a chest, with notes on what to look for, however it's just a starting point, nothing beats getting out to shops and museums and looking at hundreds of pieces until you can "feel in your bones", when a piece is right.

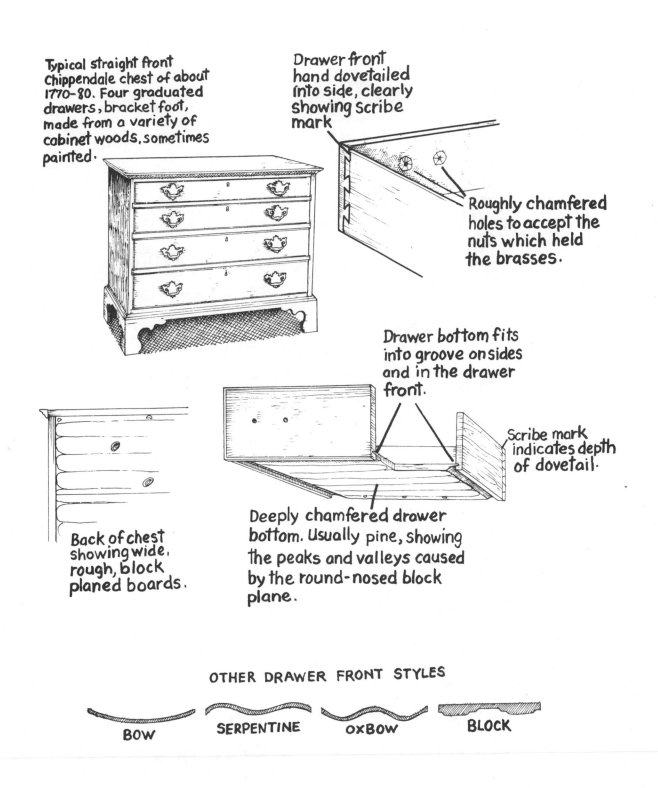

Typical straight front Chippendale chest of about 1770-80. Four graduated drawers, bracket foot, made from a variety of cabinet woods, sometimes painted.

Drawer front hand dovetailed into side, clearly showing scribe mark

Roughly chamfered holes to accept the nuts which held the brasses.

Drawer bottom fits into groove on sides and in the drawer front.

Scribe mark indicates depth of dovetail.

Back of chest showing wide, rough, block planed boards.

Deeply chamfered drawer bottom. Usually pine, showing the peaks and valleys caused by the round-nosed block plane.

OTHER DRAWER FRONT STYLES

BOW   SERPENTINE   OXBOW   BLOCK

59

FURNITURE HARDWARE

The appearance of antique furniture is greatly improved by the correct hardware. Unfortunately, much of the furniture that has survived does not have it's original brass. Either through damage or updating most of the furniture you'll see for sale will have incorrect hardware. On the next couple of pages, I've shown the correct hardware for specific periods and I've mentioned in the chapter on refinishing where good reproductions are available.

1720
1750

Queen Anne

Chippendale

Queen Anne escutcheon

1750
1775

escutcheon

1690
1720

Tear drop handle

1760
1800

Late Chippendale
and Hepplewhite

Tear drop escutcheon

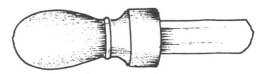

WOODEN KNOB
TAVERN TABLE TYPE

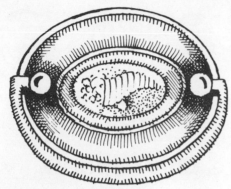

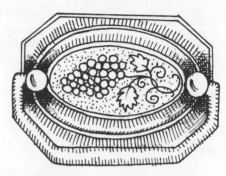

Hepplewhite Oval

Sheraton oblong

 1785
1800

 1800
1830

matching escutcheon

Sheraton escutcheon

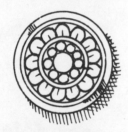

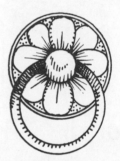

Rosette

lion's head

Ring pull

Wooden
mushroom
knob

Last four about 1805
to 1830. Lion's head +
wood knob primarily
empire.

Pine
Blanket Chest
18th cent.

The first thing the
Pilgrims must have
done when they
stepped down off the rock
was make a blanket chest and
their descendants continued the
tradition. It's practically impossible not to
run across two or three varieties on even
the most casual antique hunt. The fact
that they're readily available shouldn't
dissuade you from acquiring one. The
blanket chest is indeed a true antique that
still serves it's original purpose admirably.
　　　They come in many variations on
the basic form, which is simply a box
with a hinged lift top. You'll find them with

a varying number of useable drawers and with false drawers on the face of the box section. You'll find many painted in nice old colors and some with decoration. If you find one decorated with some exceptional folk art, make sure the paint is dry before you shell out to much money.

Antique blanket chests date from the earliest settlement thru the 1840's, the most common today being the ones from the late 18th and early 19th century.

Typical blanket chest hinges

18th cent. forged iron

cast iron early 19th cent.

COTTERPIN   STRAP

Blanket Chest
Pine, about 1790

A popular variation on the simple
six board chest is the one drawer version
shown here. It has as its' finish attractive
graining in yellow and red, which may
sound a bit garish, but time has softened
the effect, until now it is quite pleasant.

65

Sea Chest
Pine
early 19th cent.

Really nothing more than an early sea bag, used to hold the sailors effects while at sea. Made of pine, sometimes decorated, occasionally with the painting of the sailors ship. This type of rope carrying handle, is called a "Becket" and was often used on sea chests.

67

Blanket Chest
18th cent.

Here's a New Hampshire blanket chest that dates about 1760 or 1770, the finish is the original old red color. The wood, both primary and secondary is pine.

The drawers are graduated in size as they should be, but in the wrong direction. Normally the smallest is the top drawer, but every now and then you will run across a country chest of drawers that reverses the order. The bracket foot is a good high one of the fish tail pattern which adds to the style.

The brasses are not original, but follow the outline of the originals. The two bottom drawers are false. The top lifts to reveal the storage area.

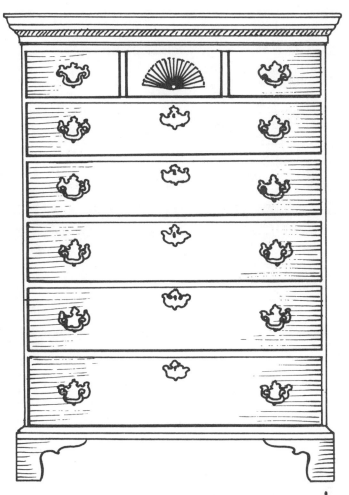

Maple 6 drawer chest
1760-70

Probably New Hampshire, fan
carved in center of top drawer.

chippendale four drawer chest
about 1780

A good looking, late Chippendale
style cherry chest. The corners of the
chest are finished off in what is
referred to as a lamb's tongue. The
bracket feet are in the ogee style. The
brasses are original.

Queen Anne
Highboy

1750-60

A flat-top
highboy of
the Queen
Anne period.
Made from
native
hardwoods,
usually
maple or cherry,
fan carved
center drawer.

71

Queen Anne
Lowboy
1750-60

Often made as a companion
piece to the highboy. The
demand is greater because
of their smaller size, but the
price on either one runs
into the thousands.

73

Country Hepplewhite Chest
1790-1800

This particular chest is all pine, now finished in a satin varnish, but traces of old red paint indicate its original finish.

Many simple chests of this type were made from available native woods and false grained to imitate something more exotic, evidently an early attempt to "keep up with the Joneses."

Today a chest with its original graining intact will bring twice as much money as one that has been refinished. This is true of most antique furniture and a good point to consider before getting out the paint remover.

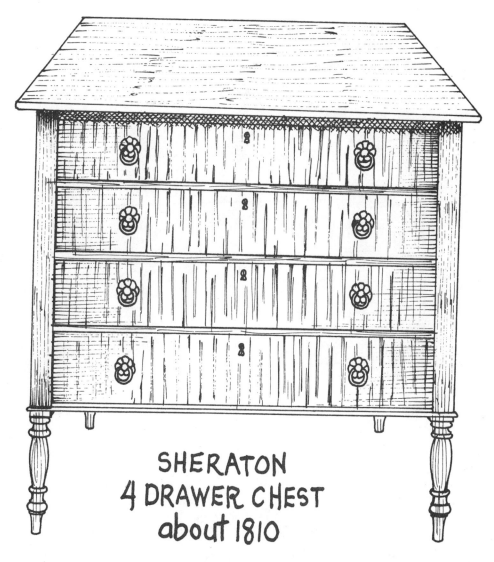

SHERATON
4 DRAWER CHEST
about 1810

Cherry with curly maple drawer
fronts, a nice combination. Ring pull
brasses and short turned leg. The sides
are paneled to prevent splitting.

75

EMPIRE
4 DRAWER CHEST
about 1825

This Empire chest is cherry and while not exactly rare, it is unusual. Most are mahogany and crotch grain mahogany veneers and fall more readily into an urban furniture classification.

76

77

CHIPPENDALE
DESK ON FRAME
about 1770-80

An all pine desk on frame, finished in an old dark varnish. This particular desk is from the coast of Maine and was used in an office as a work desk. The square Chippendale legs are refered to as Marlborough legs.

79

SHERATON
SECRETARY DESK
about 1810

   Made in Rhode Island in the early 19th century. The top section lifts off, as it does on most secretaries, for easier moving.

   The cupboard section is divided into pigeon holes and small drawers and finished in an old red color. The present brasses are empire lion-heads with a ring pull. They are of course, not original, the first brasses appear to have had round back plates. The total height of the piece is about 63"

Chippendale
Slant front
desk
1760-70

A popular desk in today's
market. Generally made of maple or cherry
although walnut was sometimes used, especially
in the Pennsylvania area. A good point to
remember is that the slides that support
the desk lid on antique desks must be pulled
out by hand, they do not operate mechanically
with the desk lid as on a modern desk.

STANDING WALL CUPBOARD 18ᵗʰ cent.

Unlike the massive architectual corner cupboards built into 18ᵗʰ cent. dining rooms to display fine china, these simple pine cupboards were kitchen pieces, designed to hold the humbler day to day ware. Has nicely paneled doors with "H" hinges.

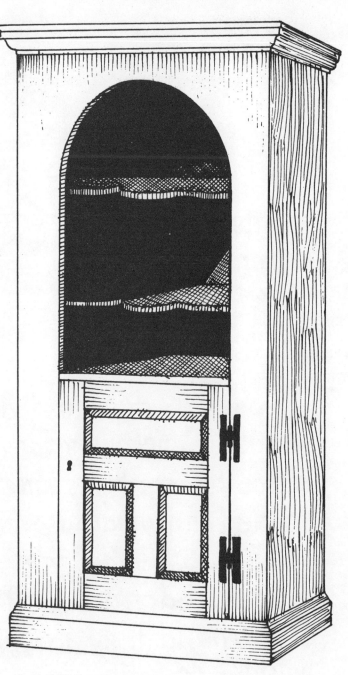

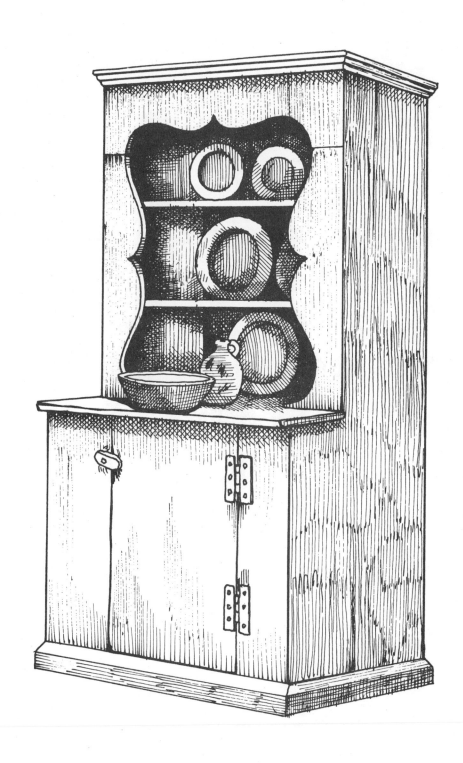

83

Pine Pewter Cupboard
last half of the 18ᵗʰ cent.

The top section is cut in an ogee scroll, which gives a stylish touch to an otherwise plain piece. The door swings on "H" hinges.

Hanging
Corner Cupboard
Late 18th cent.

All pine, paneled
door, shelves
for flip glasses
below. Found
in Cape Cod.

Small Standing
Cupboard

early
19th cent.

Only about
two feet
high.
Original old
blue paint.
The sides cut
out to form
a simple
"bootjack" base.

87

Standing Cupboard
mid 19th cent.

This pine cupboard from Northern Maine has painted on it a veritable orchard of fruit trees in their natural colors. The case is painted a soft bluish-green, the door frames and drawer fronts are not painted but are stained a reddish-brown, the two large drawers are decorated with oval landscape paintings. It's one piece construction of inch thick pine makes it the kind of piece you don't plan on moving more than once.

It's large, as many of these mid 19th cent. cupboards are, standing almost 7 feet high by 4 feet wide.

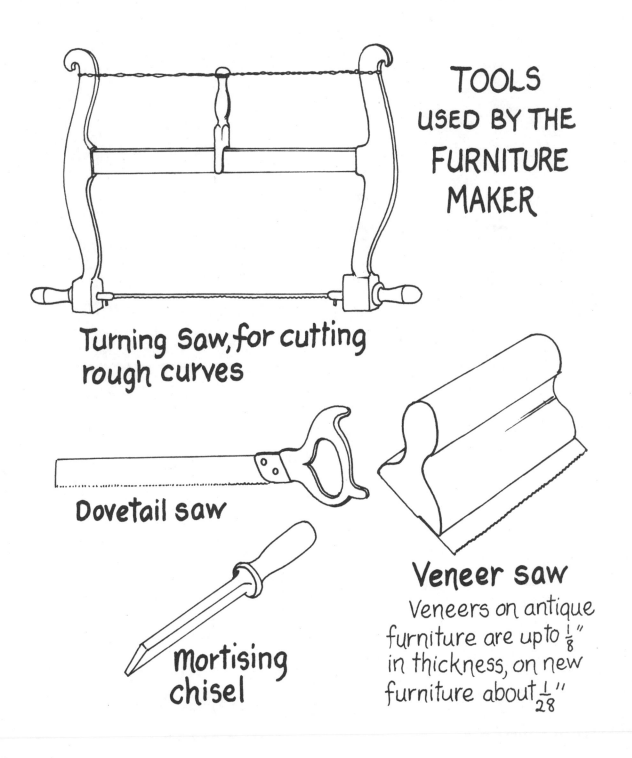

TOOLS USED BY THE FURNITURE MAKER

Turning Saw, for cutting rough curves

Dovetail saw

Mortising chisel

Veneer saw

Veneers on antique furniture are up to $\frac{1}{8}''$ in thickness, on new furniture about $\frac{1}{28}''$

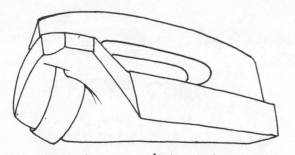

Tool used to shape the seats of Windsor chairs.

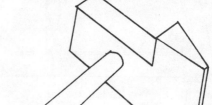

The draw knife was a common early tool for rounding and shaping.

Not really a hammer, but a burnishing tool to press excess glue out from between the veneer and what it was being applied to.

The furniture maker, of course had many more tools in his tool chest, other types of saws, turning chisels, scrapers, brace and bits, and planes to name a few. The study of early tools is a fascinating one that often leads people to specialize in collecting only tools.

Spring Pole Lathe

Here's how the old time cabinetmakers did all those fancy turnings on chair and table legs without the aid of a lot of expensive power tools. A leather thong went from a springy pole, passed around the part being turned and through to a treadle on the floor. The craftsmen worked the treadle with his foot while resting the chisel on the bar and made a cut on every downstroke. The other type of lathe was called a big wheel lathe, it was similar in most respects except it was driven by a wheel 7 feet in diameter connected by a rope to a pulley which spun the headstock. The wheel of course had to be turned by an apprentice, persumably one with a lot of stamina.

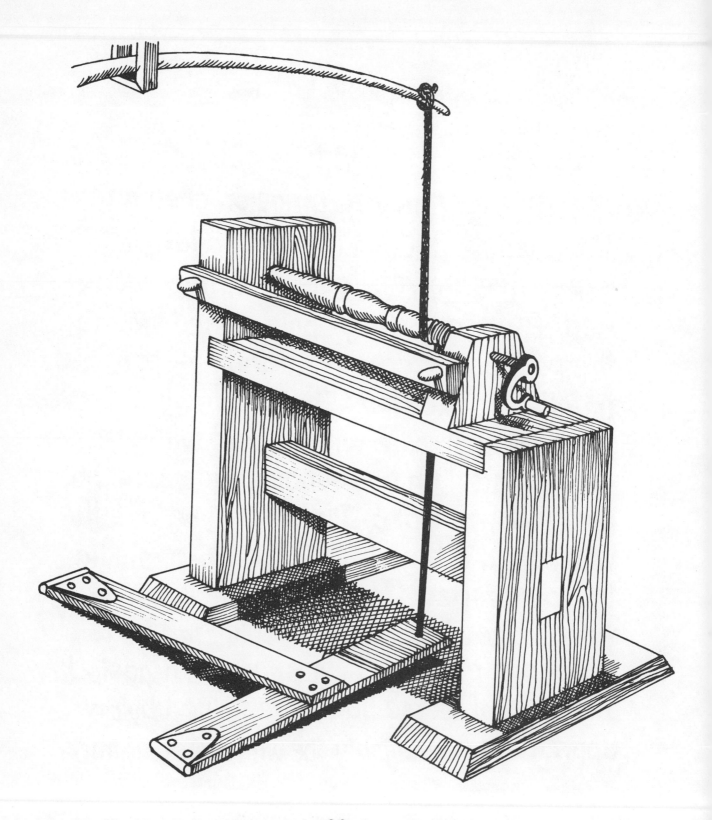

92

FURNITURE
At Low Prices.

A very large assortment of good Furniture now on hand, will be sold by the subscribers at

PRICES BEFORE UNHEARD OF.

All who may want anything we keep, will do well to call and look, at least. We have Sofas, Lounges, Bureaus, Center-Tables, Bedsteads, Chamber setts, Wash Stands of all kinds,

MAHOGANY, BIRCH, MAPLE,

Oak, Walnut, Kitchen, and Windsor Chairs, Spring Mattresses of three or four patterns, very cheap, Tables of all kinds,

EXTENSION TABLES VERY LOW,

Looking Glasses, Picture Frames of all kinds, Mattrasses of all kinds on hand or made to order, Old Hair Mattrasses made over as good as new.

UNDERTAKING !

We keep on hand a very large assortment of Coffins of every description, furnish Shrouds, Scarfs, Carriages, and everything necessary for the interment of the dead,

AND, AT VERY LOW PRICES.

We are just completing another splendid Hearse, which will give us

Two Hearses equal to any in the State,

which we shall use on all occasions where our services are required, *without extra charge.* From our experience of many years in the business, we are confident we can give perfect satisfaction in all cases where called on.

E. QUINTARD & SONS.

Norwalk, March, 1862.

An advertising broadside from
a Norwalk, Connecticut cabinet-
maker of the last half of the 19th
century. He evidently made a very
complete line of furniture
that, according to his ad, he
was practically giving away.
If you weren't interested in
his furniture he was also
equipped to bury you at prices
so low you could hardly
afford to pass it up.

REFINISHING

The least expensive and perhaps most satisfying way of buying early furniture is "in the rough". You'll save because the dealer hasn't put any of his time or money into restoring the piece, most satisfying because you'll be turning a derelict piece of furniture into something truly beautifull (hopefully). Your friends, who think you're crazy for buying this junk (or is it junque) and not being aware of the scraping, rubbing, cursing and swearing that went on in your basement, will be suitably impressed as you pass off your labors with a casual "Oh, it was nothing."

The first problem with buying "in the rough" antique furniture is arriving at some sort of definition of the term. If the condition of a piece is to decrepit then its value as an antique after extensive restoration will be severly diminished, and you would be well advised to pass it in the first place.

For the purpose of demonstration, let's assume you have purchased a country Hepplewhite four drawer chest "in the rough." With your discerning eye you recoginized it's clean, simple lines through several coats of lumpy house paint, the last being a coat of glossy pink enamel, with decals of little yellow ducks all over the drawer fronts and huge glass knobs in place of the original drawer pulls.

You snapped it up at what you figure was a bargain price (you thought you caught a glimpse of the little old lady you bought it from laughing hysterically when you glanced in your rear view mirror, but you could be wrong.) You've driven home with your prize, unloaded it from the car and deposited it in your basement and now your ready for your first refinishing job. O.K. lets go —— slowly.

First you'll need a pile of old newspapers to spread on the floor, a gallon of non-flammable, semi-paste paint remover, a sleeve of 000 steel wool and a wide putty knife. Follow the directions on the can of remover as to how long to leave each application on the surface before carefully lifting it off with the putty knife. As you work your way down through the layers of paint and approach the original finish, put aside the knife and use the steel wool, in that way you'll avoid gouging the wood underneath.

If the original finish is milk paint (probably red) it really should be left intact for the sake of authenticity. This isn't as hard to do as it sounds, because almost nothing removes it except ammonia. Commercial removers have little effect on milk paint. I personally prefer the milk paint to the thought of stripping a chest of drawers with ammonia. If you feel you must remove it, be sure to work out of doors or in a room with every window open.

At this point I would like to interject a personal opinion, please resist the urge that everyone feels when faced with a messy job like furniture stripping, and that is taking the piece to one of the commercial furniture strippers to have it dipped in a tank of boiling chemicals. It destroys in minutes the patina of the wood that took perhaps two hundred years to build-up and the softer woods come back looking like they've grown hair.

You'll have to do so much sanding on the piece I doubt that you'll save any time and what you're left with looks like a piece of brand new, unfinished furniture. Always remember the closer a piece is to original condition the better.

If it turned out that the finish on the chest was milk paint and you decided to leave it on, you don't have to varnish it, but you may. If the original finish was shellac, now removed, then you should put a protective finish on the wood.

There are several types of finish that may be applied, but I personally feel, that for ease of application and the protection given from alcohol and water stains, nothing beats a modern synthetic varnish.

Any good satin finish furniture varnish will do, a clean dry brush about 2 inches wide, not the most expensive brush, but good enough so the bristles don't keep falling out onto the wet finish. Remove the drawer pulls if you haven't already and take the drawers out of the chest so they may be varnished horizontally.

Work in a well lighted room to be sure you're not missing any spots. Don't worry about brush marks, they'll disappear in the drying. Two coats is usually sufficient, with a couple of days drying time between applications.

It's best to wait for a dry day to work, as varnish tends to dry slowly in damp weather, increasing the chances of dust settling on the piece, making for an interesting though not particulary desirable pebble-grain finish.

After the finish has dried hard its time to replace those glass knobs with the proper brasses. The original pulls probably made a slight indentation on the drawer fronts and that's your clue to the correct replacement.

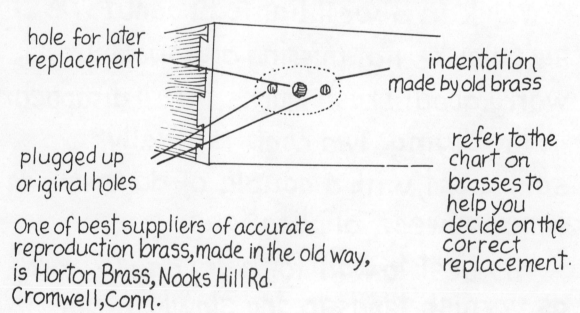

hole for later replacement

indentation made by old brass

plugged up original holes

refer to the chart on brasses to help you decide on the correct replacement.

One of best suppliers of accurate reproduction brass, made in the old way, is Horton Brass, Nooks Hill Rd. Cromwell, Conn.

Other than refinishing, the next most common problem with a chest of drawers is worn drawer runners. This will cause the drawers to stick and it also generates a fine wood dust that convinces most people that the chest is crawling with wood borers or something equally ravenous. Fortunately it's a problem that can be corrected without to much difficulty. A thin strip of pine corresponding too the amount worn off the runner is nailed on with small finishing nails, which are then counter-sunk. You'll have to do some sanding and shaving on the new wood to get the drawer to fit properly. Don't forget to soap the runners and the drawer bottoms to make them slide easily.

New wood scarved to old runner

Minor repairs to antique chairs are easily undertaken by the average collector. Loose rungs can be tightened by driving thin wedges soaked in glue into the joint. When the wedge is in as far as it will go simply trim off the excess with a single edge razor blade. Don't bother to nail loose rungs, they simply won't hold.

If a chair is very loose and rickety the best thing to do is knock it apart with a rubber mallet or a

Wedges cut to fit tightly, soaked in glue, driven in, then trimmed with razor.

padded hammer, clean off the old glue (hot water softens the old animal glue) and start over again. Keep the pieces in their correct order and using white glue put the chair together <u>all at one time</u>.when it's together, but before the glue sets, place the chair on a level surface to make sure all four legs are on the ground (having the glue set with one leg an inch shorter than the others is very depressing). This is the time to tighten up any loose rungs with the wedges. Put some weight on the seat (heavy books are good) and don't touch the chair again for a couple of days.

Putting a new rush seat in an antique chair is a common problem. It's a job that requires strong hands and a lot of patience, my advice is to have it done by an expert rather than attempt it yourself. Remember only real rush will do for an old chair, synthetic rush is an anachronism to be avoided.

Most of the problems with old tables center around warped or split tops. A badly warped table top can usually be straightened but it takes some time and patience.

The first thing to do is get the top off the table, so turn the table upside down on a rug and take a look at what's holding the top to the frame. Usually it's just four screws and when these are removed the top comes right off (unless someone has hammered in a half dozen rusty finishing nails, if that's the case, make sure all the children are out of earshot before you begin.)

Be sure to save the old screws and reuse them if possible. Nothing looks more suspicious than shiny new wood screws holding down an old top.

The next step is to strip the finish off the top and thoroughly wet the concave side. A method I've used with success is to wet several thicknesses of newspaper as well as the concave side of the top, then place the top concave side down on the wet paper with some heavy rocks on top. The time it takes for the top to level off depends, of course, on how badly it was warped to begin with.

Keep the
newspapers
wet.

When the top stays straight after it has thoroughly dried (the process may have to be repeated a few times) varnish both sides of the top to minimize the chances of it warping again.

If the top has a minor split I'm inclined to forget about it, don't try to fill it with a wood filler, the expansion and contraction of the wood will only loosen the repair and cause it to fall out.

A bad split that seriously detracts from the appearance of the table can be glued and pulled together with pipe clamps.

Start by cleaning the gap as throughly as possible, first with a vacuum cleaner, then as best you can with an old toothbrush soaked in turpentine.

When you've gotten it as clean as possible, work white glue into the split, then position the pipe clamps using pieces of cardboard to protect the wood surface. Tighten the clamps a bit at a time until the glue begins to squeeze out of the crack. Wipe off the excess with some wet paper towel and let the job dry undisturbed, for about 24 hours.

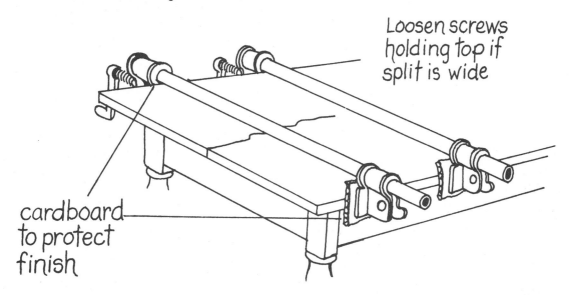

Loosen screws holding top if split is wide

cardboard to protect finish

The repairs discussed in this chapter are relatively simple and can be accomplished at home with a minimum amount of wood-working skill and simple hand tools.

More difficult restoration, such as replacing a smashed table leg, or the missing bottom turning on the leg of a chair, for instance, are best undertaken by a skilled restorer with the knowledge and equipment to do a professional job. As your collecting progresses you may find an interest developing in restoration that may lead to a workshop full of mechanical marvels to repair all the crippled furniture you cart home.

REFINISHING "TOOLS"

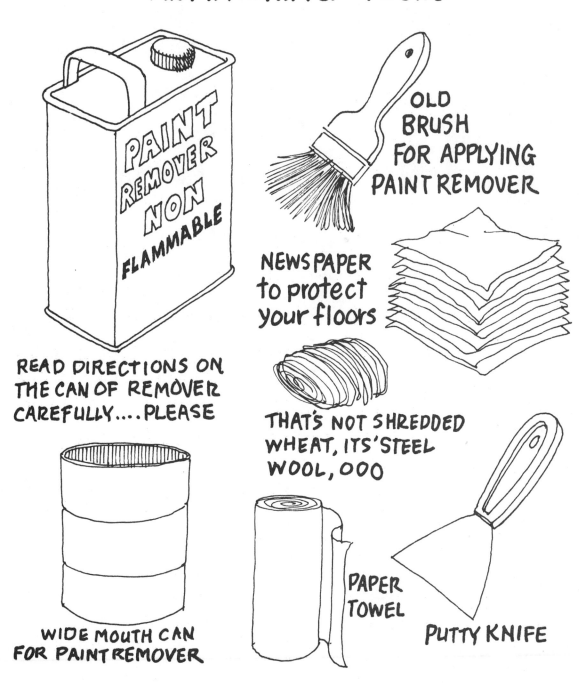

PAINT REMOVER NON FLAMMABLE

OLD BRUSH FOR APPLYING PAINT REMOVER

READ DIRECTIONS ON THE CAN OF REMOVER CAREFULLY.... PLEASE

NEWSPAPER to protect your floors

THAT'S NOT SHREDDED WHEAT, ITS' STEEL WOOL, OOO

WIDE MOUTH CAN FOR PAINT REMOVER

PAPER TOWEL

PUTTY KNIFE

ACCESSORIES 9

TIN WARE

LIGHTING DEVICES

WARMERS

FOOD SAFE

IRON WARE

WOODENWARE

BOXES

MIRRORS

CLOCKS

STONEWARE

113

Tin Heater

This painted and decorated (tole) heater dates from the middle of the 19th century. The ground color is a dark green, the stencilled flowers are gold. The heating element is a still full whale oil burner. The liquid to be heated was placed in the tin insert at the top.

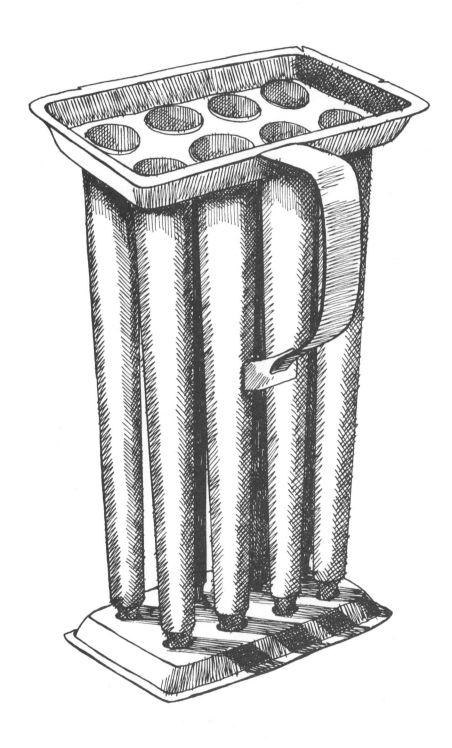

115

Tin Candle Mold
19th century

Candlemaking was, of course, an important part of life in the 18th and much of the 19th century. These tin candle molds made the operation a little easier. They were made in a variety of heights and different numbers of molds, the most common being six, eight and twelve. Large units up to fifty molds are known, these frequently were set in a wooden frame, and were probably used by chandlers, rather than at home.

117

Tin Candle box
early 19th cent.

Used to protect the families valuable candle supply. There's nothing a field mouse would rather nibble on than a tallow candle.

Tin deed box

Painted black with a cream colored band and colorful stylized leaves. A safe place for important papers. Similar boxes are still used today.

early 19th cent.

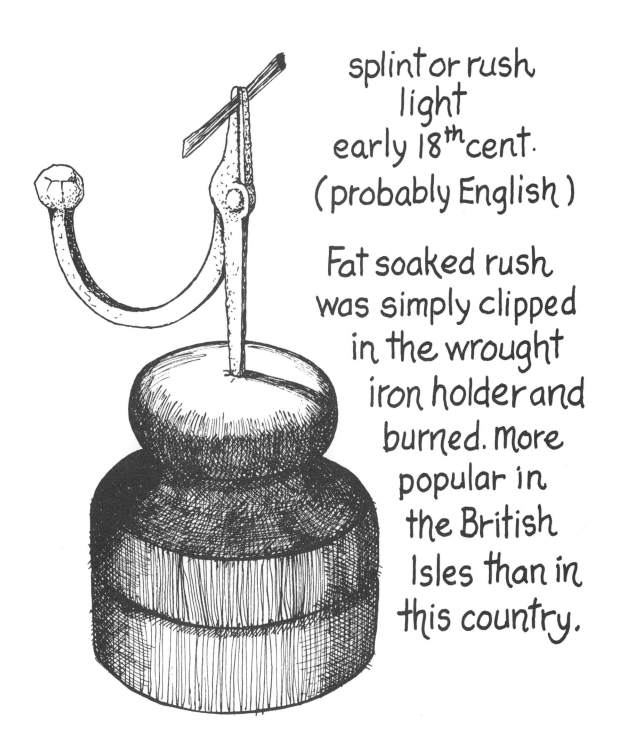

splint or rush
light
early 18th cent.
(probably English)

Fat soaked rush
was simply clipped
in the wrought
iron holder and
burned. more
popular in
the British
Isles than in
this country.

"Betty" lamp
18ᵗʰ cent.
New England

A primitive lamp form that burned tallow or lard with the aid of a wick placed in the narrow end. This type of lamp existed for centuries in most of the world. Usually hung by a spike driven into a convenient beam, they were also placed on wrought iron or wooden standards.

Queen Anne
Style

mid 18th cent.

A brass candle-
stick, probably
American, possibly
English. The same
form is found in
silver and
pewter.

121

Iron "hog scraper" candlestick

early 19th cent.

Push up device for raising candle as it burned down. Legend has it that farmers

would use the sharp saucer edge to debristle the hogs after slaughtering.

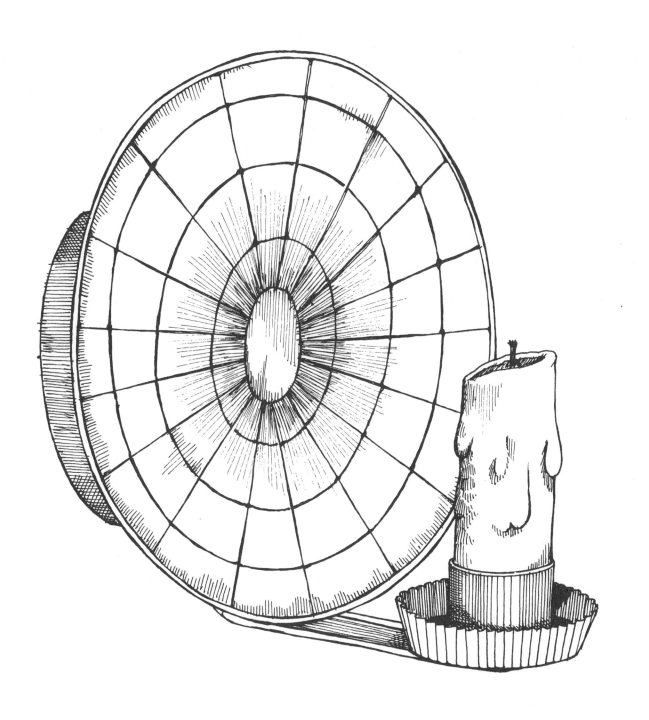

Reflective Candle Sconce
18th cent.

The sconce is tin, with shaped pieces of glass set to give a prism effect to the candlelight in an attempt to gain a little added illumination. These sconces have become quite scarce and many of the ones on the market today are of questionable age and authenticity.

Perforated tin candle lantern 18th to 19th cent.

Traditionally called a Paul Revere lantern, after the type Revere used to signal with from the Old North Church It's unlikely that the light from this type of lantern could be seen from any distance.

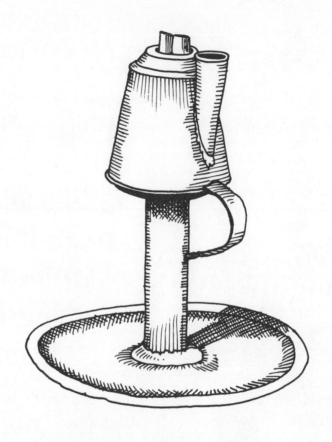

Whale Oil Lamp
double burner
early 19th cent.

Retains the basic candlestick shape

Pressed Glass
Camphene Lamp
about 1840

Camphene required
long thin burning
tubes and heavy
wicks to burn
properly. The screw
cap prevented
evaporation.

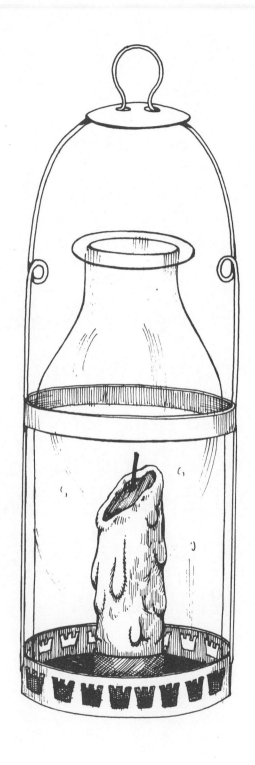

Candle
Lantern
19th
Century

Made up of wire
and tin, with a
free blown glass
bottle as the
chimney.

Candle
Lantern
19th cent.

Soldered up
by a tinsmith,
using a flip
glass as the
candle holder.

129

Candle Snuffer
and wick trimmer

early 19th cent.

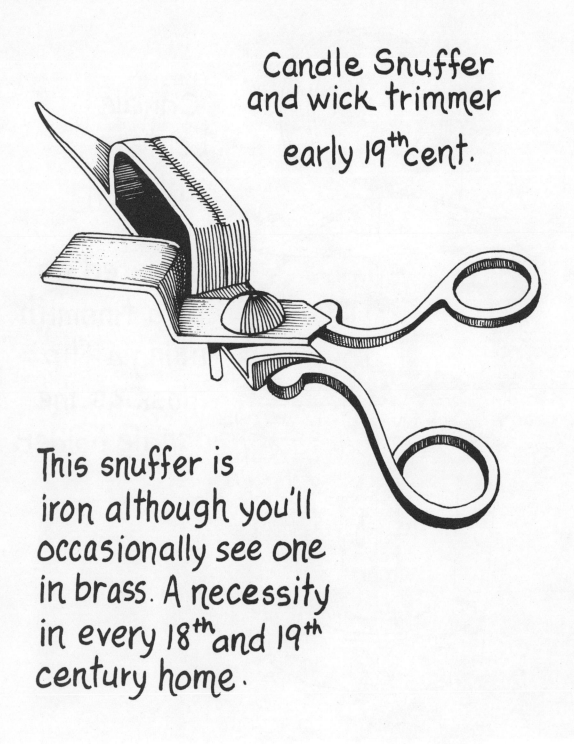

This snuffer is
iron although you'll
occasionally see one
in brass. A necessity
in every 18th and 19th
century home.

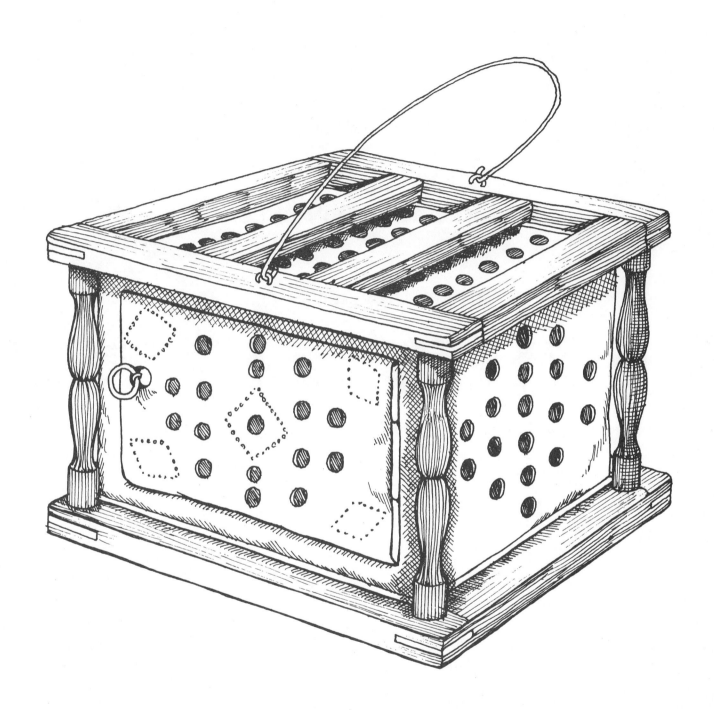

Pierced Tin
Foot Warmer
late 18th early 19th cent.

An early solution to the problem of cold feet. A tin box, held by a wooden frame with a tin warming pan inside to hold hot embers. Nice to have along under a warm robe on a cold sleigh ride.

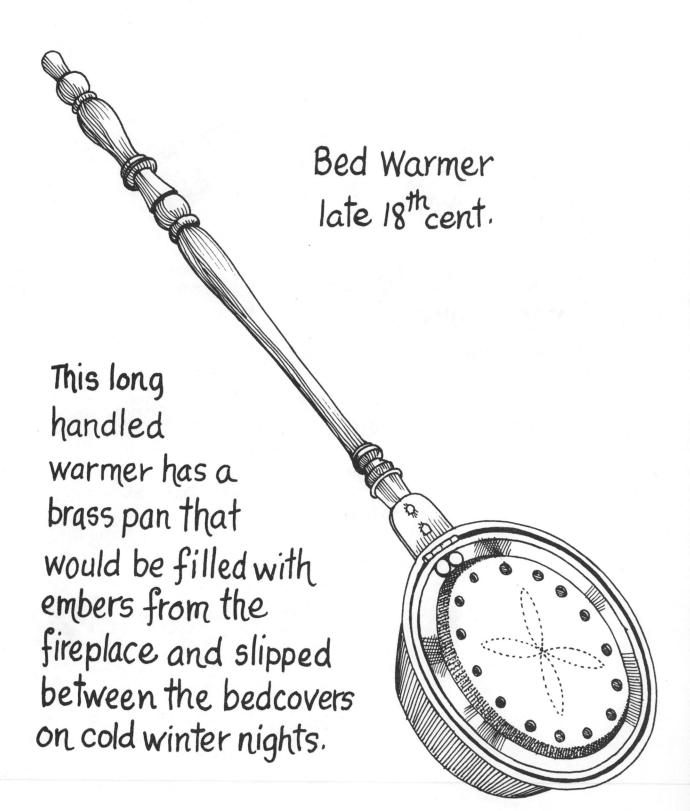

Bed Warmer
late 18th cent.

This long handled warmer has a brass pan that would be filled with embers from the fireplace and slipped between the bedcovers on cold winter nights.

Food Safe
19th cent.

You see these food
safes in various
sizes. Their
use, of course
was to keep
the flies
off the
food.

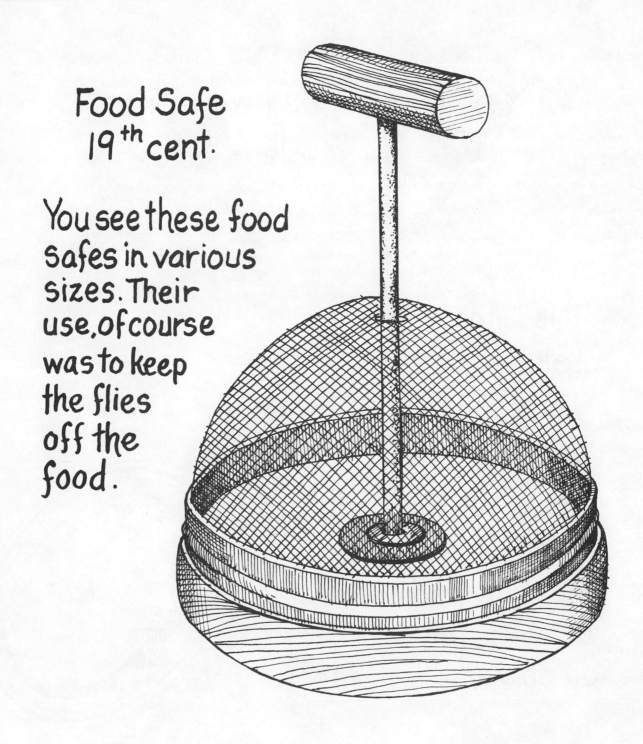

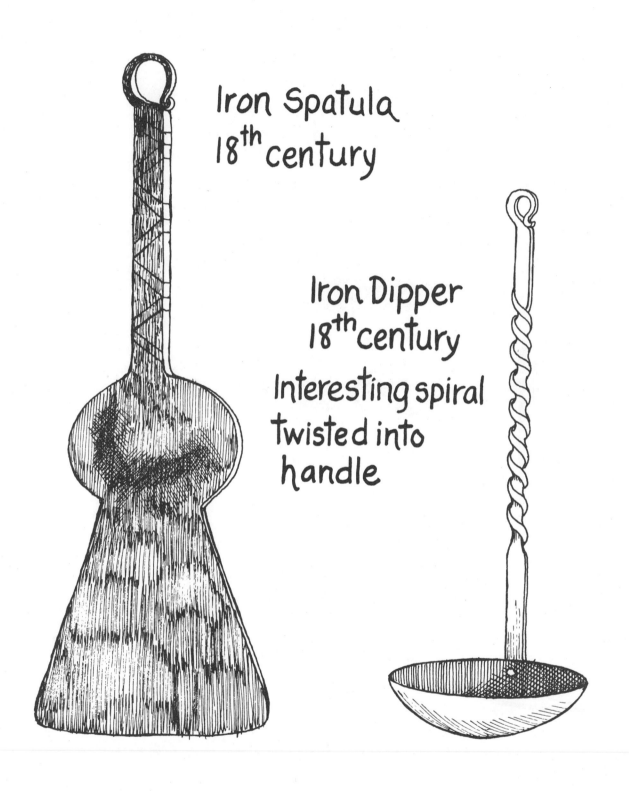

Iron Spatula
18th century

Iron Dipper
18th century

Interesting spiral
twisted into
handle

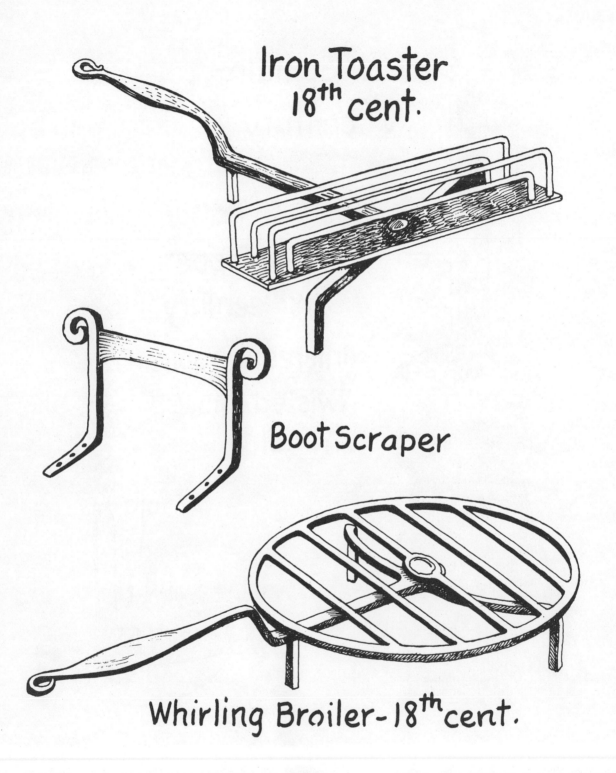

Iron Toaster
18th cent.

Boot Scraper

Whirling Broiler - 18th cent.

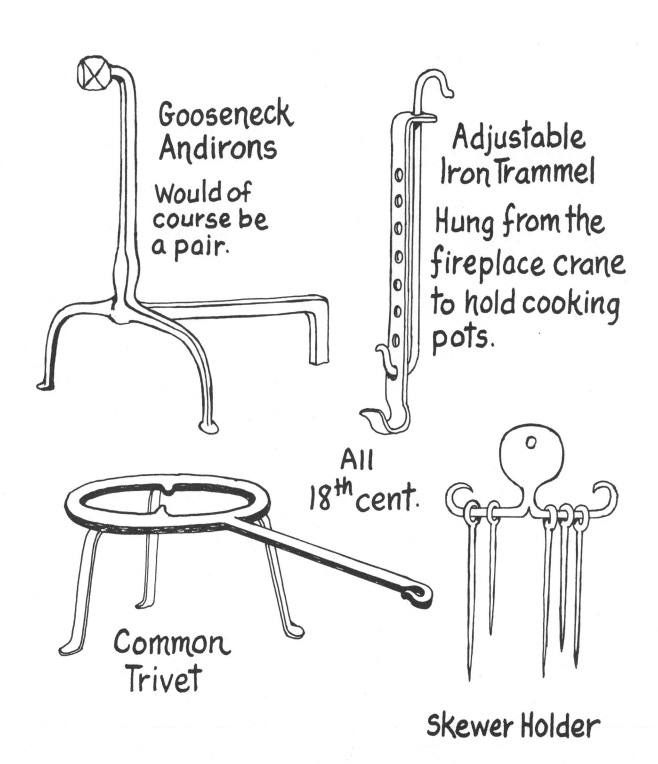

Gooseneck
Andirons

Would of
course be
a pair.

Adjustable
Iron Trammel

Hung from the
fireplace crane
to hold cooking
pots.

All
18th cent.

Common
Trivet

Skewer Holder

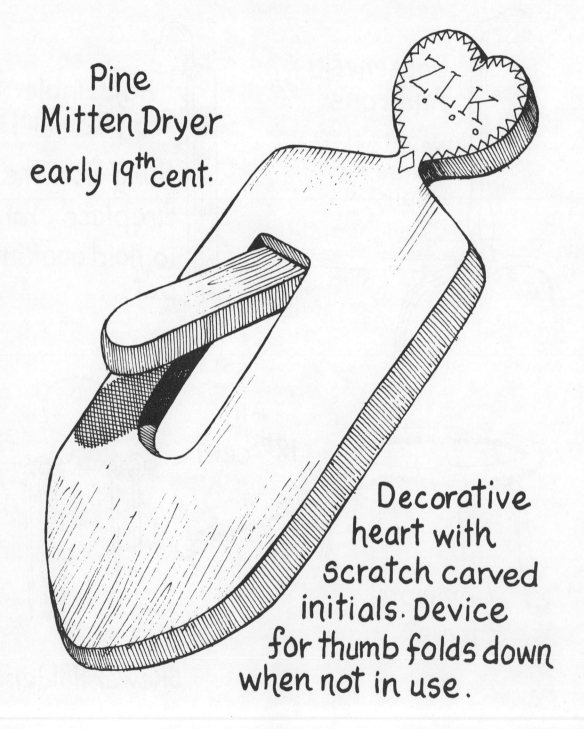

Pine
Mitten Dryer
early 19th cent.

Decorative
heart with
scratch carved
initials. Device
for thumb folds down
when not in use.

138

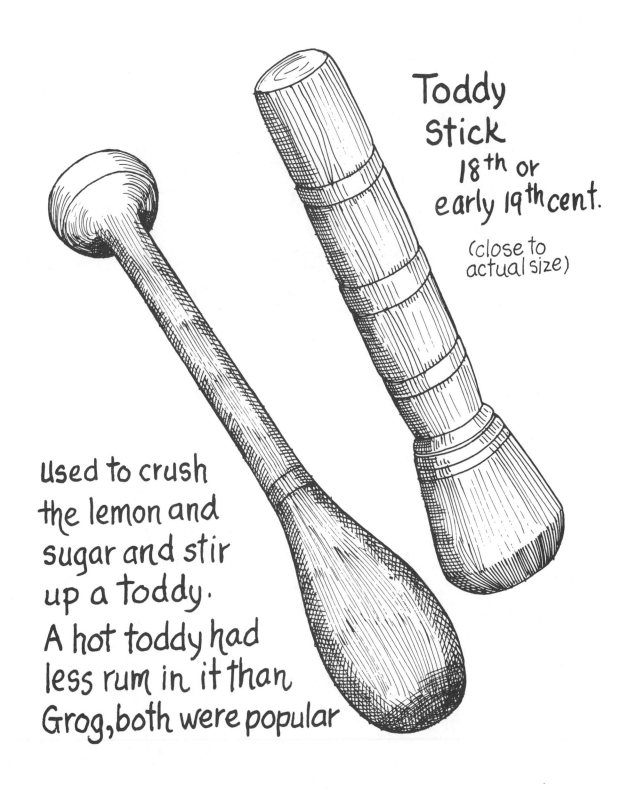

Toddy
Stick
18th or
early 19th cent.

(close to
actual size)

Used to crush
the lemon and
sugar and stir
up a toddy.
A hot toddy had
less rum in it than
Grog, both were popular

139

carved

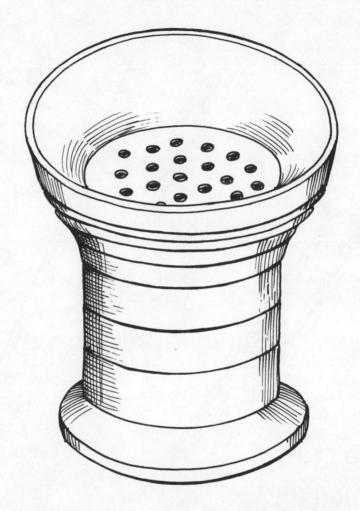

Turned Wooden Sander 18th cent.
Filled with fine sand and kept on the
writing desk to be shaken on wet
ink, much as a blotter would be
used today.

Hanging Spice Box
mid 19th cent.

Made of pine, painted
a now faded olive
green. The chunk was
taken out of the side
by a mouse who was
partial to spice
flavored pine.

Sliding Top
Candlebox
late 18th cent.

Pine, usually
painted

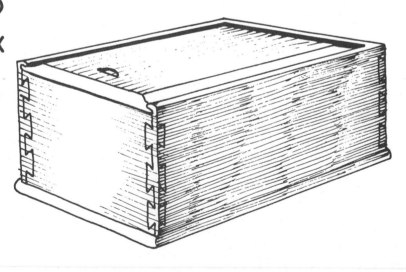

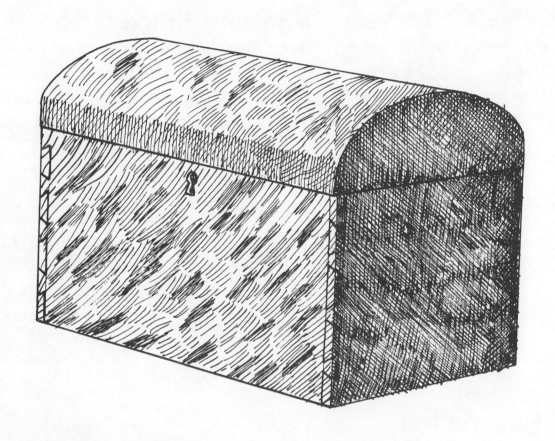

Small Dome Top Chest
early 19th cent.

Decorated in green and white paint. Many
small boxes and chests in all sizes were
made in the early days, they have always
been popular collectibles.

143

Double "Lollipop"
Candle Box

A fine example of the double "lollipop", a portion of one was broken off many years ago. The box is pine and retains most of its original red color.

18th century

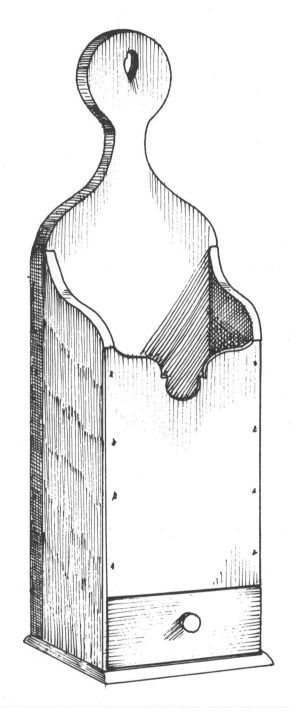

Pipe Box
18ᵗʰ cent.

Used to hold and
protect the long.
church warden
pipes. Being made of
clay they were very
delicate and easily
broken. The drawer
was for tobacco.

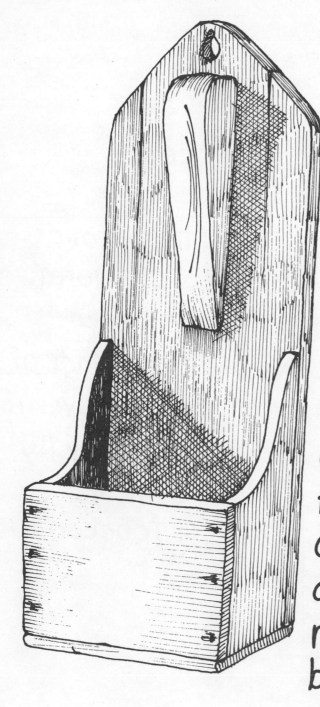

Wall Hanging
Knife box
early 19th cent.

This strictly
utilitarian piece
held pumice
used to scour
knives. The box
was taken down
off the wall and
the knives cleaned
on the wedge
of pine in the
middle of the
box.

146

Mahogany Mirror
about 1780

This type of mirror is generally called Chippendale, although the style is actually earlier. They're still available and the less elaborate glasses can still be had for a moderate price.

Looking glasses were not common in the American home of the 18th century, therefore many of the ones now for sale in this country are foreign, mostly English. It wasn't until the Federal period that American mirrors were made in any number or variety

Resist the urge to replace the wavy old glass, it's an intergal part of the mirror's originality, though it may do some odd things to the reflected image. Keep looking, you may find one that makes you look thinner.

Federal
Architectural Mirror
1800-1815

Gilded pine, reverse painting on glass
in top section.

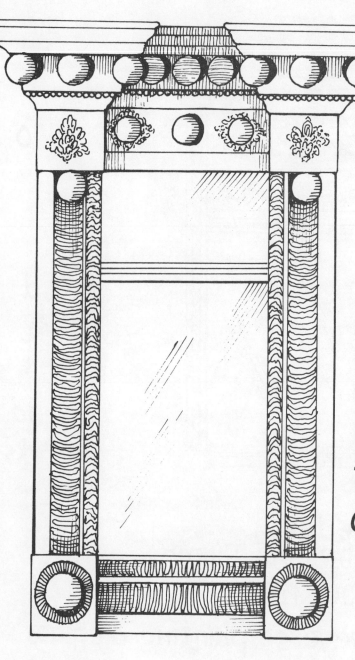

Gilded Pine
Architectural
Mirror

about 1820

Exceptionally
small, in fact
the smallest
mirror of it's
type I have seen,
only 15½" high.

Empire
Mirror-1840

All pine,
painted
yellow and
black, with
gilt on the
turnings and
corner blocks.
Charming
primitive
reverse
painting on
glass.

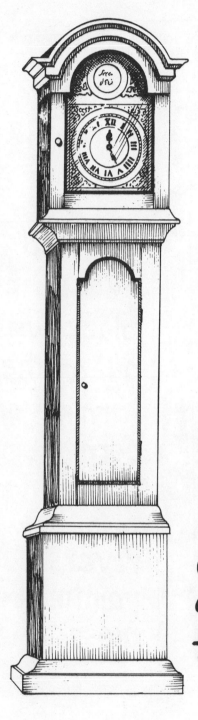

Tall Case Clock
about 1760

The maker is Matthew Reed, Norwalk, Conn. The case is cherry, the works and face are brass and probably English. There are many tall case clocks by Connecticut clockmakers available, but most date from the early 19th cent.

Pillar and Scroll
Shelf Clock

about 1820

Made by Eli Terry,
one of the many
famous Connecticut
clock makers.

30 hour wooden
movement. By 1815 clock
making was an important industry
in Connecticut.

Seth Thomas - Shelf Clock - about 1840
8 day brass movement, with alarm.
Keeps as good time today as it did
135 years ago.

Much of the American stoneware available for collecting these days is a product of the middle to late 19th century. Most of this grey salt-glazed pottery was made for utilitarian purposes (sort of an early tupperware).

Butter pots, water coolers, churns, crocks and jugs are all common examples. Occasionally you will run across some charming exceptions, such as miniature crocks and jugs, tiny tea pots, bird whistles, money banks etc. These are referred to (how accurately nobody knows) as

"End of Day" pieces. Presumably, the potter, tired of throwing chamber pots on his wheel all day, would exercise a little creativity to produce a whimsey or two for his own family.

What makes stoneware so collectible these days, is not so much the piece, but the applied decoration. Usually done in cobalt blue, or very rarely brown, the imagination of these early pot decorators seemed to know no bounds. Common decoration may consist of a single bird or flower, but that was merely a starting point for some really outlandish folk art that might include exotic animals or a whole barnyard of more common ones, people in a variety of costumes, buildings, trees, fruit, wild cartouches or any combination of the above.

The more complex and interesting decoration brings a correspondingly higher price and is more eagerly sought by advanced collectors. As a dealer friend of mine says, " I have some stoneware collectors who won't buy a piece unless the decoration is a man in a top hat, waving two American flags, standing on top of a duck." Well.... good hunting.

SOME COMMON STONEWARE FORMS

1 GAL. PITCHER

5 GAL. CROCK

CHURN

1 GAL. JUG

BOTTLE

BIRDHOUSE

CUSPIDOR

INKWELL

CHICKEN FEEDER